THE WORLD'S SILLIEST JOKES

BY
JOSEPH ROSENBLOOM
ILLUSTRATIONS BY JOYCE BEHR

Sterling Publishing Co., Inc.   New York

With love to Michelle Halfon

2 4 6 8 10 9 7 5 3 1

School Book Fairs edition published 1990
by Sterling Publishing Company, Inc.
387 Park Avenue South, New York, N.Y. 10016
This book is excerpted from *The Gigantic Joke Book*
© 1978 by Joseph Rosenbloom
Printed and bound in United States of America
All rights reserved

ISBN 0-87406-572-0

Contents

1.
Silly Questions—
Silly Answers

MUTT: Do you sleep on your left side or on your right side?

JEFF: I sleep on both sides. All of me goes to sleep at once.

ERNIE: Are you a light sleeper?

BERNIE: No, I sleep in the dark.

CUSTOMER: Do you have pig's feet?

WAITER: Yes, I do.

CUSTOMER: That's too bad. If you wear shoes, no one will notice.

CUSTOMER: Do you have frog's legs?

WAITER: No. It's a painful corn that makes me walk this way.

LEM: Is this the other side of the street?

CLEM: No, it's over there.

LEM: That's weird. The fellow over there said it was over here.

TEACHER: Lucy, what kind of leather makes the best shoes?

LUCY: I don't know, but banana peels make the best slippers.

TOMMY: Teacher, would you punish me for something I didn't do?

TEACHER: Of course not.

TOMMY: Good, because I didn't do my homework.

KNICK: What does coincidence mean?

KNACK: Funny, I was just going to ask you that same question.

What if William Toomey had a brother named Socket?

Did you hear about the silly kid who wanted to get his typewriter fixed because the "O" was upside down?

GUEST: I'd like a room for this evening.

HOTEL CLERK: Single?

GUEST: Yes, but I'm engaged to be married.

A lady brought her beaten-up car to the carwash. "Can you make my car look better?" she asked.

"Sorry, lady, we wash cars here, we don't iron them."

LITTLE BOY: Daddy, when were you in Egypt?
FATHER: Egypt? I never was in Egypt.
LITTLE BOY: Then where did you get my Mummy?

CUSTOMER: Do you serve crabs here?
WAITER: We serve everyone. Sit right down.

CUSTOMER: What is this insect in my soup?
WAITER: I wish you wouldn't ask me, sir. I don't know one bug from another.

CUSTOMER: What's wrong with these eggs?
WAITRESS: Don't ask me. I only laid the table.

FARMER: Young man, what are you doing in my tree?
YOUNG MAN: Your sign says, "Keep Off the Grass."

CUSTOMER: Could I have a glass of water, please?
WAITER: To drink?
CUSTOMER: No, I do a high diving act.

NED: I've played the piano for years—on and off.
FRED: Slippery stool?

CUSTOMER: Waiter, there is a bug in the bottom of my tea cup. What does this mean?
WAITER: How should I know? If you want your fortune told, go see a fortune teller.

"Excuse me, sir, are you reading that newspaper you're sitting on?"

IKE: How can one person make so many mistakes in a single day?
MIKE: I get up early.

SILLY: I'm thirsty.
SILLIER: I'm Friday. Come over Saturday, and we'll have a sundae.

NIT: If six-foot-tall Anna Story married Robert Short, what would happen?
WIT: It would be one way of making a long story short.

IKE: Did you hear about the cross-eyed teacher?
MIKE: No, what about her?
IKE: She had no control over her pupils.

CUSTOMER: Waiter, didn't you hear me say "Well done"?
WAITER (ignoring the undercooked and still red steak): Yes, sir. And thank you so much for the kind words. It is so seldom we hear a compliment.

NIT: What do you think of artificial respiration?
WIT: Me, I'd rather have the real thing.

DIM: Did you know there is a star called the Dog Star?
WIT: Are you Sirius?

HOTEL RECEPTIONIST: Sir, before going to your room, would you mind wiping the mud off your shoes?
YOKEL: What shoes?

TEACHER: What comes after the letter "A," Johnny?
JOHNNY: The rest of them.

Knock-Knock!
—Who's there?
A little kid who can't reach the bell.

NIT: How did you find the weather when you were away at the seashore?
WIT: It was easy. I went outside, and there it was.

DIT: Where were you born?
DOT: England.
DIT: What part?
DOT: All of me, silly.

IGOR: Why do elephants paint their toenails red?
BORIS: I don't know. Why?
IGOR: So they can hide in the strawberry patch.
BORIS: I don't believe that.
IGOR: Did you ever see an elephant in a strawberry patch?
BORIS: No!
IGOR: See? It works!

GUEST: Can you give me a room and a bath?
HOTEL RECEPTIONIST: I can give you a room, but you'll have to take your own bath.

JUDGE: Have you ever been up before me?
ACCUSED: I don't know. What time do you get up?

IGOR: What has 20 feet, green eyes, and a brown
  body with a yellow stripe?
BORIS: I don't know. What?
IGOR: I don't know either, but it's crawling up your
  back.

BABY EAR OF CORN: Mama, where did I come from
MAMA EAR OF CORN: Hush, dear, the stalk brought you.

DICK: Do you feel like a cup of coffee?
JANE: Of course not. Why, do I look like one?

WAITER: Would you like your coffee black?
CUSTOMER: What other colors do you have?

CUSTOMER: Waiter, look here, is this peach or apple pie?
WAITER: Can't you tell by the taste?
CUSTOMER: No, I can't.
WAITER: Well, then, what difference does it make?

NIT: What do you get if you cross a computer and a rubber band?
WIT: I don't know what it's called, but it makes snap decisions.

TEACHER: What comes after "G"?
SAM: Whiz?
TEACHER: No. Let's try again. What comes after "T"?
SAM: V?
TEACHER: Sam, I'll give you just one more chance. What comes after "O"?
SAM: Boy!

2.
Monkey
Business

MUTT: Fishing?
JEFF: No, drowning worms.

SILLY: Why are you swimming with your socks on?
SILLIER: Because the water is cold.

NIT: Did you get a haircut?
WIT: No, I got all of them cut.

NIT: Haven't I seen your face somewhere else?
WIT: I don't think so. It's always been between my ears.

CUSTOMER: My hair is coming out pretty fast. Can you give me something to keep it in?
BARBER: Here's an empty box.

Wise man says:
Many a true word is spoken through false teeth.

The meal in the restaurant was awful. The diner asked to see the manager. When the manager came, the diner said, "I want to compliment you on your very clean kitchen."

"Clean kitchen?" the manager asked. "Have you seen our kitchen?"

"No," the diner replied. "But it must be clean because all the food tastes like soap."

CUSTOMER: Hey, waiter, hey!
WAITER: All right sir, but we'll have to send out for it.

DINER: Waiter, it's been half an hour since I ordered the turtle soup.
WAITER: Yes, sir, but you know how slow turtles are.

TIP: I can't understand why King Arthur had a round table.

TOP: He probably didn't want to get cornered.

NITA: I just had an embarrassing experience in the kitchen.

RITA: What happened?

NITA: I opened the refrigerator and saw some Russian dressing.

DIT: Where did Larry go?

DOT: He's round in front.

DIT: I know what he looks like, I just wanted to know where he went.

REAL ESTATE AGENT: Here is a house without a flaw.

CUSTOMER: My goodness, what do you walk on?

FLIP: Speaking of inflation, have you any idea of the price of feather pillows these days?

FLOP: Not really.

FLIP: Why, even down is up.

TEACHER: Where is your pencil, Harold?

HAROLD: I ain't got none.

TEACHER: How many times have I told you not to say that, Harold? Now listen: I do not have a pencil, you do not have a pencil, they do not have a pencil . . . Now, Harold, do you understand?

HAROLD: Not really. What happened to all the pencils?

TRAMP: Could you give me a bite?

WOMAN: I don't do that sort of thing myself, but if you'll wait a moment I'll call the dog.

FLO: Is it true that an alligator won't attack you if you carry a flashlight?

MOE: That depends on how fast you carry it.

SIGNS

At a butcher shop:
HONEST SCALES—NO TWO WEIGHS
ABOUT IT

On a travel agency window:
PLEASE GO AWAY!

On a canary cage in a pet shop:
FOR SALE—CHEEP

At an auto store:
WE SKID YOU NOT

At a dry cleaners:
WE'LL CLEAN FOR YOU. WE'LL PRESS
FOR YOU. WE'LL EVEN DYE FOR YOU!

At a shoe shop window:
COME IN AND HAVE A FIT

At a hotel:
WANTED: HOTEL WORKERS. ONLY INN-
EXPERIENCED NEED APPLY.

WAITER: What's wrong with the soup?
CUSTOMER: I asked for barley soup, not barely soup.

The farmer came into the bank and asked the guard who arranged loans.

"I'm sorry, sir," the guard told him, "but the loan arranger is out to lunch."

"All right," the farmer said, "can I speak to Tonto?"

The country needed more money, so it opened a new mint which operates from 7:00 P.M. to midnight. This makes it the world's largest after-dinner mint.

DES: I just met someone who is so stupid he thinks a football coach has four wheels.
LES: How many wheels does it have?

Have you heard about the new Christmas gift item? It's a combination record player and air conditioner—for people who like to play it cool.

LEM: Down on our farm, we had a hen lay an egg six inches long.
CLEM: That's nothing much. On our farm we can beat that.
LEM: How?
CLEM: With an egg beater.

3.
Peculiar Parents

Mama Gnu said to Papa Gnu, "I want you to punish our little one. He's been bad all day."

"No," replied Papa Gnu. "I won't punish him. You will have to paddle your own gnu."

MOTHER: Do you like moving pictures?
SON: I sure do!
MOTHER: Good! Then how about helping me carry down some pictures from the attic?

ENGLISHMAN: Sir! I'll have you know my father is an English peer (pier).
AMERICAN: That's nothing. My father is an American doc (dock).

WIFE *(shaking sleeping husband)*: George, wake up!
GEORGE: What's the matter?
WIFE: I just heard a mouse squeak.
GEORGE: What do you expect me to do, get up and oil it?

LOU: My mother thinks I'm too thin.

ELLA: What gave you that idea?

LOU: She is always saying she can see right through me.

BROTHER: Father made a mistake this morning and ate soap flakes instead of corn flakes.

SISTER: Was he angry?

BROTHER: He was so angry he foamed at the mouth.

A boy climbing a tree tore his trousers. His mother said, "Now, Harold, I want you to go upstairs, take off your trousers so I can mend them, and stay in your room until dinnertime."

Fifteen minutes later Harold's mother heard a noise coming from the basement. She thought Harold had disobeyed her, left his room, and was now down in the basement. She called, "You bad boy, are you down in the basement running around with your trousers off?"

A man's deep voice came up from the celler, "No ma'am, I'm just reading the electric meter."

SAM: Father, may I have another apple?

FATHER: What! Another apple? Do you think they grow on trees?

"I finally made my son stop biting his nails."

"How did you manage to do that?"

"I made him wear shoes."

MOTHER LION: Son, what are you doing?

LION CUB: I'm chasing a hunter around a tree.

MOTHER LION: How many times must I tell you not to play with your food?

MRS. JONES: You say your son is only four, and he can spell his name backwards as well as forwards? What is is name?

PROUD FATHER: Otto.

SUZIE: Mother, where are the Andes?

MOTHER *(not listening closely)*: How should I know? If you'd put your things away where they belong, you'd be able to find them when you need them.

SON: Dad, there's a man at the circus who jumps on a horse's back, slips underneath, catches hold of its tail and finishes on the horse's neck!

FATHER: That's nothing. I did all that the first time I rode a horse.

"When are you going to mend that front fence?" the farmer's wife asked Farmer Brown.

Farmer Brown answered, "Next week when our son comes home from college."

"But what does our son know about fixing a fence?" the farmer's wife asked.

"He ought to know a lot. He wrote me that he was taking fencing lessons."

ERNIE: My grandfather was touched on the shoulder with a sword by Queen Victoria and made a knight.

BERNIE: That's nothing. My grandfather was touched on the head with a tomahawk by an Indian and made an angel.

MR. SMITH: My son is an excellent piano player. He can even play with his feet.

MR. JONES: Really? How old is your son?

MR. SMITH: Fifteen.

MR. JONES: That's nothing. My son can play with his feet, and he's only one.

FRED: Where's a phone? I've got to wire my father.
NED: What's the trouble? Can't he stand up by himself?

The mother turkey was scolding her children. "You bad children you," she said. "If your father could only see you now, he would turn over in his gravy."

BOY: Dad, what makes the thunder?
FATHER: I don't know.
BOY: Dad, what makes the snow white?
FATHER: I don't know.
BOY: Dad, you don't mind if I bother you with these questions?
FATHER: Absolutely not, son. How are you ever going to learn anything if you don't ask questions?

GHOUL FRIEND: My, how your little ghoul has sprouted up! The last time I saw him, he was only so high.
GHOUL MOTHER: Yes, he certainly gruesome.

FATHER: If you don't stop playing that saxophone, I'll go crazy!
SON: Too late, Dad, I stopped an hour ago.

4.
Sick Sick Sick

A man went to his doctor complaining about terrible neck pains, throbbing headaches and dizzy spells. The doctor examined him and said, "I'm afraid I have some bad news for you. You have only six months to live."

The doomed man decided he would spend his remaining time on earth enjoying himself. He told his boss what he thought of him and left his job. Then he took all his money out of the bank and bought a sports car, 10 new suits, and 15 pairs of new shoes.

Then he went to get himself a dozen tailored shirts. He went to the finest shirt shop he could find. The tailor measured him and wrote down size 16 neck.

"Wait a moment," the man interrupted. "I always wear a size 14 neck, and that is what I want."

"I'd be glad to do it for you sir," the tailor replied. "However, if you wear a size 14 neck you're going to get terrible neck pains, throbbing headaches and dizzy spells."

A vain lion wanted to find out why the other animals were not as beautiful as he.

First he asked a giraffe. The giraffe did not know. Next the lion asked a bear. The bear had no answer. Then the lion asked a hippopotamus, and again got no answer.

Finally, the lion met a mouse. He asked the mouse, "Tell me, why aren't you as big, as strong, and as beautiful as I am?"

The mouse looked up at the lion and said, "Well, I've been sick."

MOTHER: Son, why on earth did you swallow the money I gave you?

RODNEY: Because you said it was my lunch money.

PATIENT: Can a person be in love with an elephant?
DOCTOR: No.
PATIENT: Do you know anyone who wants to buy a very large engagement ring?

MUTT: My grandfather has a wooden leg.
JEFF: That's nothing. My grandmother has a cedar chest.

A doctor was examining the sick boy in his room. He came out of the room and asked the boy's father for a screwdriver. The father quickly fetched the screwdriver and gave it to the doctor.

The doctor went back into the sick boy's room. In a few minutes he came out again. This time he asked for a hammer and chisel.

The father rushed out and got the tools and the doctor went back into the boy's room.

In a few minutes, he came out again.

The father could stand it no longer and pleaded, "For goodness sake, Doctor, what's wrong with my son?"

"I haven't had a chance to examine him yet," the doctor replied. "I can't get my medicine bag open."

TEACHER: I excused you last week from school, Willie, because you said your aunt was dying. I saw her in the beautician's yesterday.
WILLIE: Correct. That's where she was dyeing. Now she's a blonde.

"Was I brought here to die?" asked the first Australian as he opened his eyes in the hospital.

"No," answered the second Australian. "You were brought here yester-die."

DIT: What do you want to take for your cold?
DOT: I don't know. What'll you give me?

A cowboy boasted to the sheriff that he had the best horse in the world.

"I was riding him through a lonely stretch of the country, when he stumbled over a rock. I fell from the saddle and broke my leg."

"Don't tell me," the sheriff said, "that the horse reset your leg!"

"Nope. But he grabbed me by the belt, dragged me home, and galloped five miles to fetch the doctor."

"I'm glad everything worked out so well," said the sheriff.

"Not really, that dumb horse fetched a horse doctor!"

PATIENT: Lately I've had the feeling that everyone wants to take advantage of me.
DOCTOR: That's nonsense.
PATIENT: Really? Thank you very much, doctor. I feel so much better now. How much do I owe you?
DOCTOR: How much have you got?

Psychiatrists tell us that one out of four people are mentally ill. So check your friends—if three of them seem to be all right, you're the one.

Wise man says:
Anyone who goes to a psychiatrist ought to have his head examined.

DIT: I always wear sunglasses on rainy days.
DOT: Why is that?
DIT: To protect my eyes from umbrellas.

FLIP: What was the terrible noise I heard before?
FLOP: My sister fell down a flight of stairs.
FLIP: Cellar?
FLOP: No, I think she can be fixed.

Have you heard about the amazing new discovery? It is a pill that's half aspirin and half glue—for people who have splitting headaches.

DOCTOR: Your cough sounds much better today.
PATIENT: It should. I practiced all night.

TED: I saw a doctor today about my poor memory.
NED: What did he do?
TED: He made me pay in advance.

DIT: What are you doing for your cold?
DOT: Nothing.
DIT: Why not?
DOT: Why should I? What's it doing for me?

PATIENT: Doctor, I understand that you are the greatest expert in the world for the cure of baldness. If you cure me, I'll give you anything you ask.
DOCTOR *(after examining patient)*: I have some good news and some bad news. First the bad news: I can't grow any more hair on your head. Now for the good news: I can shrink your head to fit the hair you've got.

LITTLE BOY: My father beats me up every morning.
LITTLE GIRL: How terrible!
LITTLE BOY: Yes, he gets up at 7 and I get up at 8.

DOCTOR: What seems to be the problem?
PATIENT: I eat dates.
DOCTOR: What's wrong with that?
PATIENT: Off calendars?

PRU: What is the best way to prevent diseases caused by biting insects?
STU: Don't bite any.

MOTHER *(to child)*: "If you fall from that tree and break both legs, don't you come running to me."

BIFF: My cousin swallowed a frog.
BOFF: Did it make him sick?
BIFF: Sick! He's liable to croak any minute!

NURSE: Doctor, there is an invisible man in the waiting room.
DOCTOR: Tell him I can't see him.

ROGER: First I got appendicitis, then tonsillitis, followed by pneumonia. It was climaxed with neuritis. They finished me off with hypodermics and inoculation.
DODGER: How dreadful!
ROGER: You can say that again. I thought I'd never get through that spelling test.

BIOLOGY TEACHER: Do you know that you have 60,000 miles of blood vessels in your body?
PUPIL: No wonder I have tired blood.

MUTT: How did you break your arm?
JEFF: I followed my doctor's prescription.
MUTT: How could you break your arm by doing that?
JEFF: The prescription blew out of the window— and I followed it.

CUSTOMER: Is your water supply healthy?
WAITER: Yes, sir, we use only well water.

FLIP: I'd like to tell you a joke about the measles, but I'd better not.

FLOP: Why not?

FLIP: You know how those things spread.

Health Hint:
Brush your teeth regularly with an electric toothbrush—and see your electrician twice a year.

ERNIE: Where were you born?

BERNIE: In a hospital.

ERNIE: How terrible! What was wrong with you?

ERNIE: I just swallowed a bone.
BERNIE: Are you choking?
ERNIE: No, I'm serious.

DING: I woke up this morning feeling awful. My head was spinning, and everything went around and around.
DONG: You must have slept like a top.

Wise man says:
An apple a day keeps the doctor away—if aimed right.

FLIP: I went to the optician because I saw spots in front of my eyes. He gave me glasses.
FLOP: Did the glasses help?
FLIP: Yes, indeed! Now I can see the spots much better.

WITCH DOCTOR (to sick native): "Drink this potion of ground bat wing, lizard tail, alligator scale, and hawk feather. If that doesn't work, take two aspirins twice a day."

JEKYLL: I just had my appendix removed.
HYDE: Have a scar?
JEKYLL: No, thanks, I don't smoke.

5.
Put-Downs

CLOTHING SALESMAN: That suit fits you like a glove.
CUSTOMER: Can you show me one that fits like a suit?

HORACE: I can't get to sleep some nights. I've tried all sorts of remedies, but nothing seems to work.
MORRIS: Have you tried talking to yourself?

BILL: I didn't come here to be insulted!
PHIL: Where do you usually go to be insulted?

NIT: Please call me a taxi.
WIT: Okay, you're a taxi. But to tell the truth, you look more like a truck to me.

FIRST HUNTER: Be careful with that gun. You just missed shooting me.
SECOND HUNTER: Did I? I'm very sorry.

MONA: Whenever I'm down in the dumps I buy new clothes.
LISA: So that's where you get them!

35

FIRST WOMAN: He kept my photograph over his heart and it stopped the bullet when that bank bandit fired at him.

SECOND WOMAN: I'm not surprised. Your face would stop anything.

I never forget a face, but in your case I'll make an exception.

IGOR: I trace my ancestors all the way back to royalty.

BORIS: King Kong?

When your grandfather was born, they passed out cigars. When your father was born, the passed out cigarettes. When you were born—they just passed out.

TIP: I suppose you think I'm a perfect idiot?

TOP: No, no one is perfect.

MONA: Whenever you sing, it reminds me of a pirate.

LISA: How is that?

MONA: Murder on the high C's.

IGOR: Commissar! Commissar! The troops are revolting!

COMMISSAR: Well, you're pretty revolting yourself.

PUPIL: I don't think I deserve a zero on this test.

TEACHER: I agree, but it's the lowest mark I can give you.

IGGY: Where do all the bugs go in the winter?
ZIGGY: Search me.
IGGY: No, thanks. I just wanted to know.

MRS. SMITH: Have you told your little boy not to go around imitating me?
MRS. JONES: Yes, I have. I told him not to act like an idiot.

ANDY: Did the music teacher really say your voice was out of this world?
SANDY: Not exactly. She said it was unearthly.

KITTY: How do you like my new dress? I got it for a ridiculous price.
CATTY: You mean you got it for an absurd figure.

NED: Our dog is just like one of the family.
FRED: Which one?

Wise man says:
   Better to keep your mouth closed and make people wonder if you are stupid, than to open it and remove all doubt.

TUTTI: I don't know which to go to—a palmist or a mind reader. Which would you suggest?
FRUTTI: Better go to a palmist—at least you know you've got a palm.

DIT: Is that perfume I smell?
DOT: It is—and you do!

IGGY: When tourists visit my town, they come to see me.
ZIGGY: Yes, you sure are a sight!

NIT: I wonder how long a person can live without a brain?
WIT: How old are you?

DICK: Don't you think I sing with feeling?
JANE: No. If you had any feeling, you wouldn't sing.

MUSICIAN: Why do you play the same piece of music over and over?
STUDENT: It haunts me.
MUSICIAN: It *should* haunt you, you've murdered it long enough.

She was going to have her face lifted, but she couldn't find the jack.

MUTT: I understand that fish is brain food.
JEFF: Yes, I eat it all the time.
MUTT: Oh, well! There goes another scientific theory.

"Harry learned to play the piano in no time."

"Yes, I heard him playing it that way the other day."

HORACE: Last night I dreamed I saw something in front of your house that made me very happy.
MORRIS: What was it?
HORACE: A moving van.

LEM: You remind me of a shirt button.
CLEM: How is that?
LEM: Always popping off.

SHE: You remind me of the ocean.
HE: You mean wild, restless, romantic?
SHE: No, you make me feel sick.

HE: I have music in my feet!
SHE: Yes, two flats.

He is so stupid he has to stand on his head to turn things over in his mind.

PROUD FATHER: My baby is the image of me.
BYSTANDER: What do you care, so long as it's healthy?

6.
Careers

NIT: How's your radio working?
WIT: It isn't working, it's playing.

BOSS: Please file these letters.
SECRETARY: Wouldn't it be easier to trim them with a pair of scissors?

Wanted:
Person to work on Fissionable Isotope Molecular Atomic Reactive Counters and Triple-Phase Cyclotronic Plutonium Hydrodynamics. *No experience necessary.*

LEM: What is the best way to carve wood?
CLEM: Whittle by whittle.

Did you hear about the man who lost his job as an inspector in a mattress factory? He fell awake on the job.

Did you hear the one about the chauffeur who was so stupid that when his boss told him to put water in the car, he put a bucket in the back seat?

FLIP: Do you know why the butcher put bells on his scale?

FLOP: I don't know, why?

FLIP: Because he wanted to jingle all the weigh.

BUTCHER: The lamb I got in today is excellent.

BUTCHER'S WIFE: Must you always talk chop?

NIT: Why did you become a printer?

WIT: I was the right type.

MUTT: I'm learning to be a barber.

JEFF: Will it take long?

MUTT: No, I'm studying all the short cuts.

"Believe me," the salesman said to the lady, "this sewing machine will pay for itself in no time."

"Good," she replied. "When it does, send it to me."

Did you hear about the umbrella salesman who saved his money for a sunny day?

STORE MANAGER: Aren't you the boy who applied for a job two weeks ago?
BOY: Yes, sir.
MANAGER: And didn't I say I wanted an older boy?
BOY: Yes, sir. That's why I'm back here now.

CUSTOMER: Are you supposed to tip the waiters here?
WAITER: Why, yes.
CUSTOMER: Then tip me, I've been waiting for two hours.

Did you hear about the vampire who went to sea? He signed up on a blood vessel.

FIRST GHOST: You work for a spiritualist, I hear.
SECOND GHOST: Yes I do.
FIRST GHOST: Is he any good?
SECOND GHOST: I would say medium.

NIT: Did you hear about the undertaker who buried a body in the wrong place?
WIT: That was a grave mistake.

Two stupid carpenters were building a wall when one noticed the other picking nails out of a box, nailing some in the wall, and throwing the others away. The first man thought this was rather strange and asked, "Why are you throwing those nails away?"

"Well," replied the second carpenter, "the heads are on the wrong ends of those nails."

"You dummy you!" the first carpenter shouted, "those are for the other side of the wall!"

TUTTI: Is it true that the workers in the mint have too much work to do?

FRUTTI: Yes, and they're threatening to go on strike unless they make less money.

The waitress was new and she already had dropped a load of dishes that morning. When she dropped a second load, the manager called out. "More dishes?"

As the waitress picked up the broken dishes, she said, "No, sir—less!"

WORKER: Aren't you ashamed to give me such a poultry paycheck?

BOSS: You mean paltry.

WORKER: No, I mean poultry. It's chicken feed.

TIP: I used to be a newspaper man.

TOP: What happened?

TIP: Someone stole my stand.

PILOT: Do you wanna' fly?
CO-PILOT: Sure.
PILOT: Wait a second and I'll catch one for you.

JOE: When did you decide to become a parachute jumper?
MOE: When the plane caught fire.

SHE: Are you a toe dancer?
HE: Why, no.
SHE: Then would you please get off my toes!

Did you hear about the fellow who became an astronaut? He did it because people said he was no earthly good.

MOTHER: I think our son is going to be an astronaut.
FATHER: What makes you think so?
MOTHER: I spoke to his teacher today. She said he is taking up space.

REPORTER (to ASTRONAUT): Tell me, what is the secret of space travel?
ASTRONAUT: Don't look down.

The bus was packed. When the man tried to get on, the people already in the bus refused to let him inside.

"It's too crowded, there isn't any more room!" they shouted.

"But you've got to let me on!" the man pleaded.

"Why should we? Who do you think you are, someone special?" they shouted.

"No," he pleaded, "I'm just the driver."

Did you hear about the bank clerk who climbed a tree because he wanted to become a branch manager?

Did you hear about the mad scientist who invented a square bathtub so it never left a ring?

"He was a Marine corporal, but they had to kick him out."

"What for?"

"Because he was rotten to the Corps."

JUNIOR: I'm not going back to school anymore.

MOTHER: Why not?

JUNIOR: On Monday the teacher said that four and four make eight. On Tuesday she said six and two make eight. Today she said that five and three make eight. I'm not going back until she makes up her mind.

CUSTOMER: Waiter, this food gives me heartburn.
WAITER: What did you expect—sunburn?

MOE: He must be in the watch business.
JOE: Whatever gave you that idea?
MOE: Whenever I work, he watches.

Two detectives are standing over the dead body of a man named Juan.
FIRST DETECTIVE: He was killed with a golf gun.
SECOND DETECTIVE: What is a golf gun?
FIRST DETECTIVE: I don't know, but it sure made a hole in Juan.

Wise man says:

The secret of success is getting ahead—but not a big one.

Clothes may not make the man—but a good suit has made many a lawyer.

He who keeps nose to grindstone ends up with flat face.

7.
Oldies but Goodies

Two country yokels were fishing. For three hours nei ther of them moved a muscle. Then one became restless. His companion grumbled, "That's the second time you've moved your feet in twenty minutes. Did you come here to fish or to dance?"

IGGY: Did you take a bath today?
ZIGGY: Why? Is one missing?

LITTLE SUZIE: Mother, you know that vase you said had been handed down from generation to generation?
MOTHER: Yes.
LITTLE SUZIE: Well, this generation just dropped it.

JACK: Say, Jill, how did you get that swelling on your nose?
JILL: I bent down to smell brose in my garden.
JACK: Not brose, Jill, rose. There's no "B" in rose.
JILL: There was in this one.

BIG AL: What are you doing with a pencil and paper?
LITTLE AL: I'm writing a letter to my brother.
BIG AL: But you don't know how to write.
LITTLE AL: That's okay, my brother can't read.

ERNIE: What is your pet pig's name?
BERNIE: Ballpoint.
ERNIE: Is that his real name?
BERNIE: No, that's his pen name.

GOODENOV: I woke up last night with the feeling that my watch was gone. So I looked for it.
BADENOV: Was it gone?
GOODENOV: No, but it was going.

TEACHER: What is a conductor of electricity?

LOUELLA: Why, er-r—

TEACHER: Correct. Now tell, Louella, what is the unit of electric power?

LOUELLA: The "what"?

TEACHER: Correct, very good.

ERNIE: To the right of me was a ferocious lion, on my left a tiger ready to spring, and in back and in front of me were stampeding elephants!

BERNIE: How did you escape?

ERNIE: I got off the merry-go-round.

CUSTOMER: Waiter! There is no turtle in the turtle soup.

WAITER: Of course. If you look close you'll see that there is also no horse in the horseradish.

CUSTOMER: Waiter, this soup tastes funny.

WAITER: Then why aren't you laughing?

CUSTOMER: There's a fly in my soup.

WAITER: Well, it's better than having no meat at all.

CUSTOMER: Waiter, what is this fly doing in my soup?

WAITER: It looks like the backstroke to me.

PITTER: I have a three-season bed.

PAT: What is a three-season bed?

PITTER: One without a spring.

CUSTOMER: This goulash tastes terrible.
WAITER: Our chef has been making goulash since before you were born.
CUSTOMER: Maybe so, but why did he save it for me?

FLO: What is the name of your dog?
MOE: Ginger.
FLO: Does Ginger bite?
MOE: No, but Ginger snaps.

MINI: Did you hear about the trouble in the bakery last night?
MAXI: No, what happened?
MINI: Two stale buns tried to get fresh.

HE: Do you know how to make a Venetian blind?
SHE: No, how?
HE: Stick your finger in his eye.

She nodded to the minister as he passed. "Mother," asked her son, "who was that man?"

"That is the man who married me," Mother replied.

"If that is the man who married you," asked the boy, "what's Daddy doing in our house?"

BIFF: How's your nose?
BOFF: Shut up!
BIFF: So's mine—must be the cold weather.

FLIP: How were the exam questions?
FLOP: Easy.
FLIP: Then why do you look so unhappy?
FLOP: The questions didn't give me any trouble—just the answers.

MOTHER: Now, Dexter, eat your spinach. It's good for growing children.
DEXTER: Who wants to grow children?

SNIP: I went window shopping today.
SNAP: Did you get anything?
SNIP: Yes, I bought four windows.

EKE: How do you get down from a horse?

ZEKE: Jump off?

EKE: Nope.

ZEKE: Use a ladder?

EKE: Nope.

ZEKE: Well, then, how *do* you get down from a horse?

EKE: You don't get down from a horse, you get down from a duck.

CUSTOMER: Waiter, there is a fly in my soup.
WAITER: Don't worry, the spider on the bread will take care of it.

TEACHER: What does it mean when the barometer is falling?
PUPIL: It means that whoever nailed it up didn't do it very well.

DICK: Great news! Teacher said we would have a test today, rain or shine.
JANE: What's so great about that?
DICK: It's snowing.

IKE: My brother has been playing the piano for three years.
MIKE: Aren't his fingers tired?

NED: I know someone who whistles while he works.
TED: Is he that happy?
NED: No, he's a traffic policeman.

SUZIE: Mother, I can't go to school today.
MOTHER: Why not?
SUZIE: I don't feel well.
MOTHER: Where don't you feel well?
SUZIE: In school.

DIT: I slept last night in a ten-foot bed.
DOT: That's a lot of bunk!

TIP: How can you tell the difference between ducks and geese?

TOP: A duck goes "quack, quack" and a goose goes "honk, honk."

TIP: Good. Now suppose you were hunting and a flock of birds came into sight and went "honk, honk," what would you do?

TOP: I'd pull over and let them pass.

A teacher came into the classroom and noticed a girl sitting with her feet in the aisle and chewing gum.

"Eloise," said the teacher, "take that gum out of your mouth and put your feet in this instant!"

SILLY: What is the best way to clean a tuba?

SILLIER: With a tuba toothpaste.

FRED: When I die I'm going to leave my brain to science.

NED: That's nice. Every little bit helps.

8.
Sports Spectacular

GAME WARDEN: Catch any fish?

FISHERMAN: Did I? I took out forty this morning.

GAME WARDEN: That's illegal. Know who I am? I'm the game warden.

FISHERMAN: Know who I am? I'm the biggest liar in the world.

TEACHER: Now, children, I want you all to draw a ring. (*Johnny draws a square.*)

TEACHER: Johnny, I told you to draw a ring, and you've drawn a square.

JOHNNY: Mine's a boxing ring.

DICK: Did anyone laugh when you fell on the ice?

RICK: No, but the ice made some awful cracks.

JAMES: I went out for the football team, Dad.

FATHER: Did you make it?

JAMES: I think so. At the end of the practice session, the coach looked at me and said, "This is the end."

FLAP: My brother was doing all right until they caught up with him.

JACK: I didn't know your brother was a crook.

FLAP: He isn't. He's an auto racer.

ERNIE: The national sport in Spain is bull fighting and in England it's cricket.

BERNIE: I'd rather play in England.

ERNIE: Why do you say that?

BERNIE: It's easier to fight crickets.

Sign in gym:
> THE WORLD IS IN BAD SHAPE—
> MUST YOU BE TOO?

NED: Can you skate?
FRED: I don't know. I can't stand up long enough to find out.

A fisherman had tried several different kinds of bait without getting a single bite. In disgust he threw a handful of coins into the lake.

"Okay, wise guys," he shouted to the fish. "Go out and buy something you like!"

NITA: I used to go skiing in the Sahara.
RITA: That's stupid. Whoever heard of skiing in the Sahara?
NITA: You did. I just told you.

GAME WARDEN: You can't fish without a permit.
FISHERMAN: Thank you just the same, but I'm doing fine with this worm.

Once a terrible golfer hit a ball onto an ant hill. He went over to the ant hill to hit the ball. No matter how hard he tried, all the golfer managed to do was to hit the ant hill and kill many ants. At last, only two ants remained. One turned to the other and said, "If we want to stay alive, we'd better get on the ball."

The two mountain climbers had reached the end of their exhausting journey. They were at the point of total collapse, but they had made it to the top. One of the mountain climbers turned to the other and said, "It almost cost us our lives to climb to the top of Mount Everest to plant our country's flag, but it was worth it. Please hand me the flag."

The second mountain climber stared at him with a surprised look and said, "I thought you brought it."

CAPTAIN (boasting): This boat makes twenty knots an hour.

PASSENGER: How long does it take the crew to untie them?

IKE: Did you hear about the man who went swimming in the river on Sunday? When he wanted to come on shore he couldn't.

MIKE: How come?

IKE: The banks were all closed on Sunday.

A hunter was deep in the jungle when he came upon a witch doctor pounding his drum furiously.

"What is the matter?" the hunter asked.

"We have no water," the witch doctor replied.

"Are you praying for rain?" the hunter asked.

"No, I'm calling the plumber," the witch doctor answered.

FIRST HUNTER: Where are you going with that rifle?

SECOND HUNTER: Hunting for alligators.

FIRST HUNTER: There are no alligators around here.

SECOND HUNTER: I know that. If there were, I wouldn't have to hunt for them.

FLAP: Where did you get that stuffed lion's head?

JACK: I went hunting with a club.

FLAP: Wasn't it dangerous to hunt lions with only a club?

JACK: No, the club had fifty members and they all had guns.

FIRST HUNTER: I just met a great big bear in the woods.

SECOND HUNTER: Did you give him both barrels?

FIRST HUNTER: Both barrels? I gave him the whole gun.

Did you hear about the karate expert who joined the army? The first time he saluted he nearly killed himself.

TOM: Did you ever see a catfish?

JERRY: Sure!

TOM: How did it hold the rod?

At a championship high diving contest, a spectacular dive was performed to the wild applause of the audience. Then the announcer's voice came over the loud speaker.

"Ladies and gentlemen! I have some good news and some bad news. The good news is that the judges have awarded the magnificent dive you just witnessed a perfect score. The bad news is, there was no water in the pool."

9.
Try These on a Friend— If You Dare

DING: Do you know the difference between a piece of chocolate cake and an old glove?
DONG: No.
DING: Good, then eat this old glove.

LEM: Did you ever hear the memory joke?
CLEM: No.
LEM: Sorry, I forgot it.

DIT: I haven't slept for days.
DOT: Aren't you tired?
DIT: Not in the least. I sleep nights.

"I bet I can jump across the street." *(Your friend says you can't. Walk across the street and jump.)*

LONG: Is your refrigerator running?
SHORT: Yes.
LONG: Better catch it!

BORIS: I can lift an elephant with one hand.
IGOR: I don't believe you.
BORIS: Get me an elephant with one hand, and I'll
show you.

TIP *(sitting next to an empty seat)*: Will you join me?
TOP: Why, are you coming apart?

DIT: Something happened to me yesterday that will
never happen to me again, even if I live to be a
hundred.
DOT: What's that?
DIT: I was twelve years old.

HORACE: Do you believe in the hereafter?
MORRIS: Yes, I do.
HORACE: Then, hereafter don't bother me.

"I can stay under water for ten minutes!" *(Your
friend probably will say this is impossible. Then take
a glass of water and hold it over your head.)*

FLIP: Why did the turkey cross the road?
FLOP: I don't know, why?
FLIP: To prove he wasn't chicken.

FIRST COLLEGE STUDENT: I'm studying ancient history.
SECOND COLLEGE STUDENT: So am I. Let's get together someday and talk over old times.

LITTLE AL: I bet I can make you say "black."
BIG AL: Okay, try it.
LITTLE AL: What are the colors of the flag?
BIG AL: Red, white and blue.
LITTLE AL: I told you I could make you say black.
BIG AL: I didn't say black.

IGGY: Did you hear about the owl who went "tweet, tweet" instead of "who, who"?

ZIGGY: No. Why did he go "tweet tweet"?

IGGY: Because he didn't give a hoot.

JOE: If you were walking in a field and you didn't have a gun and you saw a bear heading for you, would you keep on walking—or would you run back into town?

MOE: I'd run back into town.

JOE: With a bear behind?

"If frozen water is iced water, what is frozen ink?"

"Iced ink."

"You do?!"

HORACE: I can prove that you are not here.

MORRIS: I don't believe you.

HORACE: I'll show you. Now, tell me, are you in New York?

MORRIS: No.

HORACE: Are you in Los Angeles?

MORRIS: No.

HORACE: If you aren't in those places, you must be someplace else, right? And if you're someplace else, then you aren't here.

"Is Frank Walls there?"
  "No."
"Is Pete Walls there?"
  "No."
"Are there any Walls there?"
  "No."
"Then what holds the roof up?"

BIFF: Have you heard? Have you heard? It's all over the building.
BOFF: What's all over the building?
BIFF: The roof.

JEKYLL: Did you hear about the boy and girl vampire who couldn't get married?
HYDE: No, what happened?
JEKYLL: They loved in vein.

"There were eight morons: do, re, fa, so, la, ti, do."
  "Hey, what happend to 'mi'?"
"Sorry, I forgot about you."

10.
Whoppers

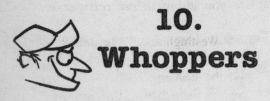

IGOR: What happens if you don't pay your exorcist?
BORIS: You get repossessed.

Zeke, the owner of the local general store, was the meanest, most insulting man in town.

One day a man walked into his store with a duck under his arm. Zeke said to him: "Say, what are you doing with that pig?"

"Are you crazy!" the man replied. "Can't you see this is a duck, not a pig?"

"I wasn't talking to you," Zeke said. "I was talking to the duck."

BIFF: When you yawn, you're supposed to put your hand to your mouth.
BOFF: What? And get bitten?

PASSENGER: What good is your timetable? The trains are never on time.
GUARD: And how would you know they were late if it wasn't for the timetable?

A woman opened her refrigerator door and found a rabbit inside.

"What are you doing in my refrigerator?" she asked.

"Isn't this a Westinghouse?" the rabbit wanted to know.

"Yes," said the woman.

"Well," replied the rabbit, "I'm westing."

Sign in a real estate office:
LOTS FOR LITTLE

TUTTI: Did you ever see a cowslip under a bush?
FRUTTI: No, but I saw a horsefly over a hedge.

A tramp knocked at the door of an inn named "George and the Dragon."

"Could you spare a poor man a bite to eat?" he asked the woman who answered the door.

"No!" she screamed, slamming the door.

A few seconds later the tramp knocked again.

The same woman answered the door.

"Could I have a bite to eat?" said the tramp.

"Get out, you good-for-nothing!" shouted the woman. "And don't you ever come back!"

After a few minutes the tramp knocked at the door again.

The woman came to the door.

"Pardon," said the tramp, "but could I have a few words with George this time?"

Two men were riding on a train for the first time. They had brought along bananas to eat on the trip. Just as they began to peel the bananas, the train entered a dark tunnel.

"Have you eaten your banana yet?" cried the first man.

"No," replied his friend.

"Well don't touch it!" warned the first man. "I took one bite and everything went dark."

LEM: Where do you bathe?
CLEM: In the spring.
LEM: I didn't ask you when, I asked you where.

TV Weatherman:
The forecast for the weekend is clear and warmer with a 70 percent chance that we're wrong.

A man walking down the street saw a delivery man struggling with a large package.

"Need any help?" said the man.

"Thanks, I could use some," replied the delivery man.

They then both grabbed an end and began to struggle with the package.

After fifteen minutes, they were both exhausted.

"I guest we'd better give up," the delivery man said. "We'll never get that package on the truck."

"*On* the truck!" the man howled. "I thought you were trying to get it *off*!"

A city dweller came to a farm and saw a beautiful horse. He decided he had to have the animal. He bargained with the farmer and the farmer finally sold him the horse.

The city man jumped on the horse and said, "Giddyup!" The horse didn't budge.

The farmer explained, "This is a special kind of horse. He'll only move if you say, 'Praise the Lord.' To stop him, you have to say, 'Amen.'"

Keeping this in mind, the new owner yelled, "Praise the Lord!" whereupon the horse took off with great speed. Soon horse and rider were headed for a cliff. Just in time the rider remembered to say "Amen!" The horse came to a screeching halt right at the edge of the cliff.

Relieved, the rider raised his eyes to heaven and exclaimed, "Praise the Lord!"

PATIENT: I am not well, doctor.
DOCTOR: What seems to be the trouble?
PATIENT: I work like a horse, eat like a bird, and I'm as tired as a dog.
DOCTOR: Sounds to me like you ought to see a veterinarian, not a doctor.

MUTT: What is that book the orchestra conductor keeps looking at?
JEFF: That is the score.
MUTT: Really? Who's winning?

A lady went into a pet shop to buy a bird. She saw one that interested her. "What kind of bird is that?" she asked the salesman.

"That is a crunchbird." he replied. "Let me show you what he can do."

"Crunchbird, my paper!" the man ordered. The bird flew down and in one gulp ate up the sheet of paper. "Crunchbird, my pencil!" The crunchbird swooped down and swallowed the pencil.

"He's wonderful!" said the lady. "I'll buy him."

The lady brought the bird home. Her husband looked at the bird and wondered what kind of bird it was. He had never seen a bird quite like it before.

"That, my dear," the wife boasted, "is a crunchbird."

The husband scratched his head. "Crunchbird?" he said, "Crunchbird, my foot!"

"You need glasses," the eye doctor said.

"I'm already wearing glasses," replied the patient.

"In that case," the doctor said, "I need glasses."

BEGGAR: Pardon me, but would you give me fifty cents for a sandwich?

PASSERBY: I don't know. Let's see the sandwich.

"Tough luck," said the egg in the monastery. "Out of the frying pan into the friar."

The dog and his master were shown to their seats by the theatre usher. When the picture was over, the dog applauded loudly. As they left the theatre, the usher asked, "And did your dog enjoy the film?"

"Very much," the dog's master replied.

"Amazing!" the usher said.

"I think so, too, especially since he didn't care for the book too much."

An Indian chief was travelling back to his reservation in New Mexico when his car broke down. Not having enough money to continue his trip, he climbed the nearest cliff and sent up smoke signals to his tribe to ask for money.

The tribe signalled back to find out what he needed it for.

Before the chief could answer, scientists from the Atomic Energy Commission exploded an atom bomb nearby. A vast cloud of smoke shaped like a giant mushroom filled the sky.

The tribe immediately answered back, "All right, all right, don't get so upset—we'll send the money!"

PATIENT: Doctor, I have a tendency to get fat in certain places. What would you recommend?
DOCTOR: Stay out of those places!

TUTTI: Do you have trouble making up your mind?
FRUTTI: Well, yes and no.

A young lady went to a fortune-teller to have her fortune told.

"I will answer two questions for you for five dollars," the fortune teller said.

The young lady paid the fortune teller but asked, "Don't you think five dollars is a lot of money for two questions?"

"Yes it is," answered the fortune-teller. "Now what is your *second* question?"

Their little baby was very quiet. It never spoke. They were pleased while he was still a baby, but as he grew up they began to worry because he never once made any sound. Finally, when the child was eight years old and had never spoken, he suddenly said, "Pass the salt, please!"

Shocked, the father asked, "How is that in eight years you never once spoke a word?"

"Well, up to now everything was all right."

"Want to get close to something that has a lot of money in it?"

"Sure!"

"Go across the street and lean against the bank."

HE: Would you like to see me walk into that lion's cage and put my head in his mouth?

SHE: Yes.

HE: And I thought you were a friend of mine!

On a cold windy day in late spring, a snail started to climb a cherry tree. Some sparrows in a nearby oak laughed at the snail. Finally, one flew over and said, "Don't you know there are no cherries on this tree yet?"

The snail thought a moment and said, "But there will be by the time I get there."

When my aunt heard that a milk bath is good for the skin, she asked the milkman for 10 gallons.

"Do you want it pasteurized?" the milkman asked.

"No," said my aunt, "up to my knees would be fine."

FLIP: Why do you take a cane to bed with you?
FLOP: In case I walk in my sleep.

DRIP: After I learned the Indian dances the members of the tribe gave me an Indian name.

DROP: What was that?

DRIP: "Clumsy."

Ali Baba went up to the entrance of the cave and cried:

"Open Sesame!"

A voice called back:

"Says who?"

Astronauts Harry and Larry were on a space ship circling above the earth. According to plans, Harry would leave the space ship to go on a 15-minute space walk, while Larry remained inside.

When Harry tried to get back into the space ship, he found the door was locked. He knocked. There was no answer. He knocked louder. Still no answer. He pounded with all his might. Finally, he heard Larry's voice inside the space ship, "Who's there?"

GERMAN BOY: Tell me, what is your telephone number?"

GERMAN GIRL: 9999999.

GERMAN BOY: All right, then don't!

FATHER BEAR: Someone has been eating my porridge.

MOTHER BEAR: Someone has been eating my porridge.

BABY BEAR: Someone has been eating my porridge, and it's all gone!

GRANDMA BEAR: I wish you'd all stop complaining. I haven't even served the porridge yet.

"Open wide," said the dentist. "Good grief! You've got the biggest cavity I've ever seen, *the biggest cavity I've ever seen!*"

"You don't have to repeat yourself," snapped the patient.

"I didn't," said the dentist. "That was an echo."

DOCTOR: Have your eyes been checked lately?
PATIENT: No, they've always been plain brown.

The tribal chief was about to cook his captive for dinner.

"By the way," the chief asked, "what kind of work do you do?"

His captive explained that he was an assistant editor.

"In that case," the chief beamed, "you will soon be an editor-in-chief!"

SAM (*boasting about his hunting trip*): All of a sudden I spotted a leopard.
PAM: You can't kid me, they come that way.

LEM: I went riding this morning.
CLEM: Horseback?
LEM: Oh, sure. He got back two hours before I did.

Read in the will of a miserly millionaire: ". . . and to my dear nephew Sam, whom I promised to remember in my will, 'Hi there, Sam!'"

11.
You Asked for It

What did the Scoutmaster say when his car horn was fixed?

"Beep repaired."

A pretty girl came into a dress shop and asked the sales clerk if she could try on the dress in the window.

"I wish you would," the sales clerk said. "It should be good for business."

Did you hear the one about the man who kept 100 clocks around the house because he heard time was precious?

Did you hear the one about the man who moved to the city because he heard the country was at war?

FLIP: What is the difference between a lemon, an elephant, and a bag of cement?

FLOP: I give up, what is the difference?

FLIP: You can squeeze a lemon, but you can't squeeze an elephant.

FLOP: What about the bag of cement?

FLIP: I just threw that in to make it hard.

One day as I sat thinking, a kindly voice came to me from up above saying, "Cheer up, things could be worse."

And so I cheered up. Sure enough—things did get worse.

TIP: I wish I had the money to buy an elephant.

TOP: What do you want with an elephant?

TIP: Nothing, I just want the money.

"Waiter!"

"Yes, sir!"

"What is this?"

"It's bean soup, sir."

"I don't care what it's been, what is it now?"

NIT: Would you like to hear the story about the broken pencil?

WIT: No thanks, it probably has no point.

CUSTOMER *(to slow waiter)*: Have you been to the zoo?

WAITER: No, sir.

CUSTOMER: Well, you should go. You would get a kick out of watching the snails zip by.

CUSTOMER: Waiter, I'll have grits, please.

WAITER: Hominy, sir?

CUSTOMER: Oh, a couple of dozen.

CUSTOMER: Could I have a glass of water, please?

WAITER: To drink?

CUSTOMER: No, I want to rinse out a few things.

MOTHER: Who gave you the black eye?

BOY: Nobody. I had to fight for it.

LITTLE KID: Show me a tough guy and I'll show you a coward.

BIG KID: Well, I'm a tough guy.

LITTLE KID: Well, I'm a coward.

NED: My pet kangaroo can't wait until it's the year 2000.

FRED: Why is that?

NED: It's leap year.

CUSTOMER: Waiter, I don't care for all the flies in here.

WAITER: Very well sir. Just point out the ones you don't like, and I'll put them out.

Did you hear the one about the girl who was so bashful she went into a closet to change her mind?

MOBY: Have you ever seen a fish cry?
DICK: No, but I've seen a whale blubber.

TIP: Have you ever hunted bear?
TOP: No, but I've gone fishing in my shorts.

BIFF: Isn't this a rare work of art?
BOOF: You are right, it's not well done.

Did you hear about the artist who was so bad he couldn't even draw his breath?

Did you hear about the fellow who spilled some beer on the stove? Now he has foam on the range.

Did you hear about the fellow who drank eight Cokes and burped 7-Up?

DIT: Did you hear about the florist who had two children?
DOT: No, tell me.
DIT: One is a budding genius, the other a blooming idiot.

A grandmother sent her grandson a shirt for Christmas. The only trouble was that he had a size 14 neck and the shirt was size 12. When the grandson sent a thank you note, he wrote. "Dear Grandma, Thanks a lot for the shirt. I'd write more, but I'm all choked up."

TEACHER: What is the formula for water?
JIMMY: H, I, J, K, L, M, N, O.
TEACHER: That's not the formula I gave you.
JIMMY: You said H to O.

CAPTAIN: Have you cleared the deck and scrubbed the portholes?
SAILOR: Yes, sir, and I've swept the horizon with my telescope.

Did you hear about the atomic physicist who was overworked because he had too many ions in the fire?

FIRST HUNTER: I shot one bullet and two rabbits died.
SECOND HUNTER: That's nothing. I shot one bullet and 500 frogs croaked.

HE: I hope you like the dictionary I bought for your birthday?
SHE: Yes, and I just can't find the words to thank you.

Last night I dreamed I was in a plane with a parachute strapped to my back. We were climbing to 40,000 feet where I was going to jump out and set a new world's record.

We got to 40,000 feet, the door opened, I took one step and plunged into space. I then pulled the rip cord—and guess what? My pajamas fell down!

All the little pigeons had left the nest and learned to fly but one. The mother pigeon said, "Son, if you don't learn to fly, I'll tow you along behind me."

"No," said the little pigeon. "I'll learn! I don't want to be pigeon-towed!"

NAT: My father collects things. He has Napoleon's watch.
PAT: That's nothing. My father doesn't even bother to collect things and he has an Adam's apple.

Did you hear about the new tax for hitchhikers? It's a thumb tax.

CUSTOMER: Why is this doughnut all smashed up?
WAITER: You said you wanted a cup of coffee and a
doughnut and step on it, so I did.

CUSTOMER: I'll have a hamburger.
WAITER: With pleasure.
CUSTOMER: No, with pickles and onions.

CUSTOMER: Have you any wild duck?
WAITER: No sir, but we can take a tame one and irritate him for you.

CUSTOMER: This soup isn't fit for a pig.
WAITER: I'll take it back, sir, and bring you some that
is.

IGOR: What are you making?

BORIS: A brilliant new invention.

IGOR: Ha, ha, ha, ha!

BORIS: Go ahead and laugh. They laughed at Edison, they laughed at Bell, they laughed at Geck.

IGOR: Who's Geck?

BORIS: You mean you never heard of Charles Geck?

IGOR: No, what did he invent?

BORIS: Nothing, but they sure laughed at him.

PIT: Did you hear about the formal dance in the zoo?

PAT: No, what happened?

PIT: The penguins came in dinner jackets and the monkeys wore their tails.

Wise man says:
Life is like a shower. One wrong turn and you're in hot water.

An elegant lady dressed in furs and flashy jewels climbed on board the bus. As she handed her fare to the driver she explained, "I always have my chauffeur and my car take me wherever I wish to go. However, today the car is being repaired." Then she added with a sneer, "I haven't been on a bus in years."

The bus driver looked up at the haughty lady and said, "You can't imagine how we missed you!"

NED: I have music in my very soul!
FRED: You're right. I did hear your shoes squeak.

FLIP: I saw a man-eating shark at the aquarium.
FLOP: That's nothing, I saw a man eating herring in the restaurant.

BILL: I know a man who drove a stagecoach and it didn't have any wheels.
WILL: What held it up?
BILL: Bandits.

Fay and May were talking on a park bench. Said Fay, "That sister of yours sure is a big gossip, isn't she?"

"I'll say she is," May replied. "When she comes home from the beach, her tongue is sunburned."

Once upon a time there was a girl named Goldie. One day she was walking in front of her house when she saw three little children passing by without any clothes on. She quickly shoved them into her house and locked the door. The name of this story is "Goldie Locks In The Three Bears."

ERNIE: I was going to tell you the story about the picture window, but I changed my mind.
BERNIE: Oh please tell me.
ERNIE: No, I think you'd only see through it.

GOODENOUGH: Why do you think people are always taking advantage of Dracula?
BADENOUGH: Because people never give a sucker an even break.

Sherlock Holmes, that master detective, was sitting in his favorite chair smoking his pipe and reading a book when he heard a knock at the door. It was his loyal friend and assistant, Doctor Watson.

"Ah, good morning, Watson. Don't you find it a bit warm to be wearing your red flannel underwear?"

Doctor Watson was astonished by his brilliant stroke of deductive logic. "Holmes," Doctor Watson said, "how on earth did you guess I was wearing my red flannel underwear?

"Elementary, my dear Doctor Watson. You forgot to put your pants on."

Sign in front of a cemetery entrance:
DUE TO A STRIKE
GRAVEDIGGING WILL BE DONE
BY A SKELETON CREW.

PAM: You should hear my new portable radio. Last night I got Mexico.

SAM: That's nothing. I just opened the window and got Chile.

IGOR: I spent 10 hours over my history books last night.

BORIS: You really studied, didn't you?

IGOR: Who said anything about studying? The books were under my bed.

CUSTOMER: Waiter, I'm in a hurry. Will the pancakes be long?

WAITER: No sir, round.

Sign on a watch repair shop:
   IF IT DOESN'T TICK—TOCK TO US

DIT: I dropped my watch.

DOT: Did it stop?

DIT: What did you expect it to do, go through the floor?

JULIET: Romeo, oh, Romeo, wherefore art thou, Romeo?

ROMEO: Down here in the flowers. The trellis broke.

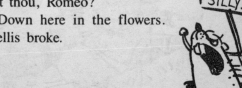

Index

94